# Pathway to Purity:
## A Practical Guide for Men

**Will Riddle**

3rd Edition

# Contents

# INTRODUCTION

Often when talking to men, we talk generically about "sin" when we all know that the main sin that affects most men is sexual. Lust is the epidemic of our age, and the struggle of men since the dawn of time. If we were to really get raw and practical in church situations we would talk specifically about freedom from sexual sin, not just tiptoe around it. If you are struggling with lust, you shouldn't be too surprised that you're not free yet, because it will take focused help to really get free. I wrote this book so that the average guy who wants to be free can be better equipped on that journey. You're not alone.

I'm speaking here from experience not theory. These are the lessons I've learned on my own journey for freedom. Some of these lessons are things people told me but I chose to learn the hard way. I hope you choose the easy way. These are keys that you need to stop losing and start winning. As I have looked at different resources, and compared notes with others on the journey of freedom, I have felt the burden to bring together into a very short guide some of the most important things that everyone seeking sexual wholeness should know. Most of these things are said somewhere else by someone, but my goal is to bring them all together in a short and easy to digest format to help your journey.

## THE STRONGHOLD

The first thing to realize is that although every man deals with the issue, not everyone has a bondage or stronghold in this area. For some men, lust is a minor life distraction that can be controlled with a moderate amount of effort. They might have to refocus after seeing a pretty girl, and be careful about how they carry themselves, but with a reasonable amount of work, these men are able to stay free from masturbation, pornography and inappropriate relationships with women. Chances are, that's not you or you wouldn't be reading this book.

On the other hand, if you haven't gotten the victory yet, this book *is* for you. You might be slipping every week or two and think it is "no big deal," or you might be might be out of control going from binge to binge, but regardless you are seeking freedom that you haven't been able to attain.

For many men, reasonable amounts of effort don't seem to have much effect. You might be looking at your peers wondering if they are free and if they are how they can be free when the fight is so hard. You've made legitimate efforts for freedom, but you just can't seem to walk in victory. Dealing with lust seems can seem like wrestling an impossibly strong dragon. The harder you fight, the harder and more hopeless it is. It seems unfair that God would ask you to tame such a massive beast as just part of your basic Christian life. And it seems amazing that any man could live free. When you look over the fence at these "normal" guys you just have to wonder, "How are they doing it?" Don't worry about those other men. I'm here to tell you that it can be done, and you can do it.

Freedom does not mean you will never in your life be tempted by lust again, it means that you will no longer be hopeless and trapped in the cycle of lusting and acting out. You can be free of the stronghold and be "normal."

This should be a liberating revelation. Don't look over at some guy who doesn't struggle and get discouraged. He may have had very different background, experiences, and makeup than you do. For some guys, moving the lust mountain amounts to Olympic training. It is discouraging if you look over at some guy crushing the weights that you can barely lift. Just accept where you are and start fighting your own fight. As God rewires you, it's going to get easier.

If you are a Spirit-filled Christian, there is a good chance you have been looking at this problem as a demonic oppression. There is almost certainly demonic activity associated with your bondage and that will need to be dealt with, but Charismatic ideas of deliverance almost always center on a singular encounter that looks at things like generational curses, past experiences, etc. They leave out all of the other aspects of a permanent transformation.

You need to look at your problem holistically to get free, and to get delivered because sexuality is a part of how you were created. In that process, you may confront and find freedom from demonic forces, but your focus should be on growing to be an overcomer. To get free and stay free, you must grow and learn to master your sexual desire.

## THE ROLE OF BEING SINGLE

I wrote this book to every man, not specifically to married or single men. When you are single it is easy to think that being married will solve the problem, because after all, at least then you will have some legitimate means of release. The Bible does say for this reason that it is better to marry than to burn with lust. (1 Cor 7:9). God gave you sexual desire to push you toward marriage, and so it's natural that it is going to be harder to stay free if you are not married.

However, you should be aware that while getting married will help take the edge off *if you have a good relationship with your wife*, it will not fix the problem. Some of the periods of abstinence you have to go through in marriage, such as when your wife gives birth, can be effectively just as long as if you were single. It is also true that during the "honeymoon" phase of any relationship you will feel like you have conquered lust but this phase of the relationship always ends, even if it takes a few years. At the end, you will find yourself back to square one, except married.

Therefore, it is best to look at this battle not in terms of your relationship status, but in terms of what you have to do to walk in freedom regardless of where you are in life. As you learn a new lifestyle and way of thinking, you can be free regardless of your status.

## How to Use This Book

Most men aren't going to read a long book, so I didn't write one. That means that I'm giving you just an overview in each area. I'd rather you have a general idea about everything you need to know than have you get stuck on chapter one and never hear the rest. Each chapter in this book addresses one important lie that is keeping you in bondage. You may only have a few of these problems or you may have all of them. This means that I'm not going too deep. Some of these areas really require a much longer treatment. If something hits you, you will need to drill deeper, take time and work it offline. This includes directly seek help from others around you, and consulting longer resources which address the specific issues you are dealing with.

The other thing many men won't do is take time to answer the questions at the end of each section. I know because I hate response questions myself, but part of getting free is doing things you've never done. To get the most value out of this book, you need take the time to write out answers to the questions at the end of each section. Part of learning is reflection and reproduction, and that's what writing answers to the questions will do.

# "It's Not a Big Deal"

Because of the prevalence of lust in our culture, it is easy to tell yourself that "It's not a big deal," but hardly anything could be more wrong. If you have read much of the Bible, one thing should be very clear to you: sexual sin is one of the most central themes of the entire Bible. And not only is it a central theme, it is a scary one. Plagues breakout because of sexual sin, people are stricken with disease, and killed and kicked out of churches because of it. There is no way around the fact that God wants a pure and holy people.

For most of us, this goes without saying, so for those who are already under conviction, I'm not trying to beat you down, but for some portion of Christian men, a healthy reminder is needed. 1 Corinthians 6:9-10 puts it in very plain terms:

> Do you not know that the unrighteous will not inherit the kingdom of God? Do not be deceived: neither the **sexually immoral,** nor idolaters, nor **adulterers**, nor men who practice **homosexuality**, nor thieves, nor the greedy, nor drunkards, nor revilers, nor swindlers will inherit the kingdom of God.

In the book of Galatians Paul says it again this way:

> The acts of the flesh are obvious: **sexual immorality**, impurity and **debauchery**; idolatry and witchcraft; hatred, discord, jealousy, fits of rage, selfish ambition, dissensions, factions and envy; drunkenness, **orgies**, and the like. I warn you, as I did before, that those who live like this will not inherit the kingdom of God.

There is not really any getting around it, if you are living a sexually immoral lifestyle, do not expect to be in heaven. And just in case, that wasn't clear enough, in Revelation it says this:

> But as for the cowardly, the faithless, the detestable, as for murderers, the **sexually immoral**, sorcerers, idolaters, and all liars, their portion will be in the lake that burns with fire and sulfur, which is the second death.

Some of us have embraced doctrines which use God's grace or mercy to make light of sexual sin, but that is not the idea found in the New Testament. You must escape its grasp if you want to be part of God's family.

This is not to mention all of the consequences in this life. Even in the "best case" scenario, you will suffer from things like:

- A guilty conscience until you come clean

- Your ministry and opportunities with God will be capped

- If you are married, your wife will usually not understand, and will go through a lot of negative emotions, perhaps taking them out on you.

- If you are not married, you or the women you are sexually involved with will either go through a lot of emotional pain, or become hardened and uncaring about others.

You would be very fortunate if these are the only consequences you experience, however. Many cases are not the "best case" scenario. Here are the kinds of consequences that men are going through every day because of sexual sin.

- If you are married, sexual sin can destroy your marriage. You may end up divorced, and your children living with a man you don't even like, while you get to visit them only occasionally. You may lose your children's respect or even a relationship with them.  Oh and most likely you will pay large sums for most of your adult life in "child support" which your ex will use any way she wants, such as pay for her getaways with the other man, or to buy his weed.  Meanwhile, you will scrape by and be put in jail if you miss a few payments.

- If you are not married, you may end up having a baby with someone you don't love.  She may kill the baby before it is born with an abortion, whether you like it or not.  Or you may end up having to put your child up for adoption, because you aren't ready to be a father.  Or you may end up forced to marry the wrong woman.

- If you do something with someone under the age of 18 and you are over the age of 18, you may end up doing prison time.  And if that happens, you will be branded a sex offender for the rest of your life.  It will be nearly impossible for you to get a job or even find a place to live.  You may not be a pedophile, but you will be treated like one.  Your parents or other family members may disown you.  And if you do time in prison, it could be dangerous there for you because they don't like pedophiles there.

- If you are in ministry, you will be taken out of ministry.  You will lose the respect of all of your friends and peers.  You will be forced to find a job doing something else, which if you are a minister, you might not have other skills to do, and could find yourself working the lowest of jobs.  This is also true if you are a teacher, counselor, or other helping profession.  Your career will be over.

- If you are a public figure, Satan will use your sin to bring mockery on the name of Christ.

- If you use your work resources to access pornography, you may be fired.

- Depending on the circumstances of sexual contact, you may get a disease.

I know this sounds dramatic, but it's not. I have observed men dealing with all of these things in real life. You need to think about what you're doing. You think you can control it, but it will control you and take you down the path to destruction. No one starts down the road of lust thinking that they will destroy their lives, but many end up doing exactly that. Listen to the wise words of Proverbs 6:27: "Can a man scoop fire into his lap and not be burned?" No. If you scoop the fire of lust into your life, you will be burned. If you don't deal with lust, eventually it will deal with you.

I'm telling you all of this to sober you up. You need out and you need to do *whatever it takes.* Until you have that kind of resolve and commitment, you're not going to succeed.

## Application Questions

1. Have you been taking sexual sin as seriously as the consequences warrant?

2. What would you do differently if you did take it more seriously?

3. What consequences are you likely to experience if you do not get control of your sexual desire?

# "I'M NOT AN ADDICT"

It can be hard to think of yourself as an "addict" because of all of the baggage that comes with it. Are you really *that* bad? Aren't you just doing what all men do? Putting yourself in the same category as someone who is putting a needle in their arm can seem like an extreme comparison. Aren't you just being a guy?

Forget about the baggage that comes with the term "addict," and let's just talk about how sexuality actually works. For a man, sexual thoughts release very powerful chemicals in your mind– these are in fact the same chemicals that are released in people who have a drug addiction. What you are doing when you fantasize about a woman, look at porn, or otherwise act out, is giving yourself a hit of a powerful and addicting drug. It just so happens that this drug is built into your own body.

Because it is built-in, sexual addiction is one of the very hardest addictions to beat. Even when you want to be completely clean, you are literally only one *thought* away from getting high. In the movie *Thanks for Sharing*, which I highly recommend, the mentor character, played by Tim Robbins, says that sex addiction is like "having the crack pipe wired up to your arm," and I think that's actually a pretty fair description of what is going on.

Even though you can't see the substance you are addicted to, and even though it is native to your body, the substance is real, and it is an addiction. Thinking about it this way will help you. You are trying to live a sober life just like an alcoholic or any other addict. Living a sober life in your case means not dosing your brain with dopamine, and that means not thinking any thought which would excite you.

Therefore when Jesus challenges us in Matthew 5:28 that even lusting after a woman is the same as adultery, He is actually giving you a very practical tip: the battle is in your mind, and you cannot be free as long as you entertain those thoughts.

## WIRED

A lot more is known now about how the brain works and how pornography affects the brain than was known even a few years ago. One of the things that we now know is that the male brain continues to develop until you are around 26 years old. This is important because it means until that age, your brain gets wired in a certain way. Whatever pathway you choose for pleasure becomes the "go to" pattern throughout your life.

I never touched drugs or alcohol even in college. Therefore, for me, drugs and alcohol are simply not very interesting. I'm not saying it would be impossible for me to develop an addiction, I'm just saying that it has no particular interest to me, and that is partly because I didn't grow up drinking. On the other hand, men that I have known who fit the pattern of being alcoholics, generally started drinking in their teens, and just continued the pattern as they got older. It became the go-to way to deal with emotional difficulty or challenge. They formed the pathway of addiction when they were young and therefore their brains are wired toward that addiction when they need comfort or relief.

If you are reading this book, it is very likely that you started on pornography or sexual promiscuity as a teenager and have continued since then. You are hard-wired. This doesn't mean there is no hope, but it does explain one of the reasons why you might have more difficulty than some of your peers. In prayer one time, I asked God to take me back to before it was an issue, and he showed me how even before I was a teen, certain things happened in my life that were designed to start the addictive thought processes. The more sexualized your upbringing was, the harder things are likely to be for you. The older the tree is, the harder it is to chop down. I think of this in several broad categories:

**Sexually Violated**: If you were sexually abused or otherwise had sexual experiences at a very young age, then your entire worldview about sex is likely to be warped. Your childhood innocence was aborted and the non-sexual bonds you were supposed to feel growing up were polluted. Love, relationship, and comfort are equated with sexuality.

If you are in this category, there is also almost always significant demonic activity which is driving your life off the cliff. These kinds of experiences can also create other problems like unwanted same-sex attraction, gender identity, sexual fetishes and compulsions. Among the other things described in this book, you should seek special ministry and counseling to forgive and be delivered. Even once you have done this, though, you still need to go through the process of learning what it is like to have loving, non-sexual relationships, and that may take a long time.

**Pre-Pubescent:** Maybe you were not sexually abused as a child but you started sexual involvement early. The normal time for you to develop sexual interests is during puberty, starting around 13-15 years old. If you started developing sexual interests or experiences before this, you are going to have a harder time getting free because the bondage is deeper.

**Puberty:**  This is the normal time for you to become sexually interested and aware.  If you started struggling with masturbation and pornography around this time, your experience is about average.  Unfortunately, depending on how much you gave into that, a lot of your brain development was wiring you for addiction.

**Late Bloomer:**  Some men are either very well sheltered by their family, or they are naturally "late bloomers" who for whatever reason do not have much sexual interest or opportunity until after high school.  My experience is that these men are often the best off in the area of lust.  During the brain's natural development, it did not get hard-wired for sex as strongly as most men.

I asked God at one point to take me back to how I thought and felt before I had a problem.  Sadly, he showed me that although there was a time in my young life that I did not think sexually, the experiences that led to my addictive thought patterns began very young.  While seemingly innocent or cute, a series of things that were little at the time were all part of developing a worldview that being with a girl who was attracted to me was the end-all, be-all of life.

I found this both daunting and relieving.  It was daunting because I realized how much rewiring would be needed to be free, but it was relieving because at least I knew why I was having such a hard time.  If your tree started growing crooked really early, you shouldn't be discouraged that you're having so much harder of a time than other men around you.  Wherever you started, God is going to heal you if you do not give up.

THE WAR IN YOUR MIND

When it gets down to it, what you are dealing with is a set of *pleasure pathways*.  You have certain sets of thoughts that are intoxicating for you. Freedom means breaking these pleasure pathways down. Someone who loves alcohol sees it as something that will bring relief and pleasure to his life. For someone who is sexually addicted, you have a variety of thoughts which do the same thing. Again, the main difference is that the drug is in your brain. As soon as you start down the pleasure pathway, you brain fires up and is ready to dose you with the drug.

This means that the *war is in your mind*. Ultimately you are not fighting an external battle related to accountability or how easy it is to get the drug, you are fighting the thoughts that lead you there in the first place. Whenever you think a lustful thought, you give yourself a huge dose of drugs, and that is naturally going to lead to acting out in some way. You need to move upstream to the thoughts themselves. When you refuse to indulge them, the addiction process stops.

On the flip side, when you watch pornography or engage in sex outside of marriage, you are doing exactly the opposite. You are supercharging the addiction, and connecting it more directly to sin. That is why one of the first things you must do is stop those outward activities. When you stop the outward activities, it is like stopping the pour of gasoline on a fire. It won't put the fire out, but it will certainly help get it under control.

You need to replace unhealthy thoughts with healthier thoughts. That's where the freedom is. When you come back to the place where you are thinking healthy thoughts about women all the time, and refusing to indulge addictive thoughts, you will actually feel the addiction slowly disappearing. Changing these thoughts is not an easy quick-fix process. It takes time, commitment and focus, but you can do it!

## Application Questions

1. Think about someone you know who is addicted to drugs or another other vice: Do they chase the high? How does sexual sin in your life function in a similar same way?

2. How and when did your sexual addiction begin? Ask God to bring you back to the time or times when sexualization took over or became the prime source of comfort in your life.

3. What are you doing that super-charges your addiction? Are you ready to make a commitment to stop?

# "LIFE'S A PARTY"

The American ideal of childhood is basically one continuous party. It starts out with outlandish, all-day birthday parties loaded with extreme amounts of sugar, and then folds in to the endless entertainment of hyper-addictive computer games, TV, and generally anything a child wants. Apart from all the other problems this causes, it is a foundational problem beneath the lust issue.

Our addiction to fun even comes out in our church culture. We love what is big, and exciting, and flashy. We love it because that's the way we were raised. And so of course the kinds of messages we get are really exciting. They give us the quick fix that we were trained to love. Have a lust problem? No problem, just three easy steps. Have a financial problem? No problem, just name it and claim it  Never mind hard work. That's for people who are "unspiritual."

If you have a serious struggle with lust, more likely than not, your upbringing involved a lot more fun than work. Because, after all, sex is the ultimate form of fun. If you are addicted to fun, it's hard not to be addicted to sex. In fact, this is exactly what happened when Israel went to worship the Golden Calf: "The people sat down to eat and drink and rose up to *play*" (Exodus 32:6). Their addiction to fun led them into an idolatrous sex party. After all, nothing is more "fun" than sex. Contrary to what our culture has come to believe, fun is not the meaning of life.

## LIVING SOBER

If you are an American, the chances are that you are living high. Sugar, video games, thrills, drugs, quick fix religion. Anything but hard work. If you want to get out, you will have to learn to live sober. And living sober can seem a little bit boring at first, I do confess. But living sober means becoming a world changer instead of a couch potato.

I first discovered this when I noticed that a friend of mine who does not struggle with lust was very productive. When he is bored, he works. He doesn't have any other vices either. He just works a lot. Another friend told me that she quit drugs by joining an intense exercise club. In other words, they learned to love the feelings that come with being sober.

We often think that being sober is just a way of saying you are not on drugs, but it is really a much broader term. Being sober means not being swayed by emotional high, and being OK with it. It is a lifestyle and way of seeing the world, much bigger than any one drug. This is one of the reasons why some people have an "addictive personality." It is because they only know how to live high. The drug of choice can change, but the high stays the same. How do you know if you are a sober person? If you never get bored, then the chances are you never get sober either. You need to learn what it is like to live without being high. It will probably feel boring at first, but don't be discouraged, that's actually part of the process. As you get used to living sober, your brain chemistry will rewire and sober will be the new normal.

There is a reason why God cursed the ground under Adam: to work it. Work is God's natural solution for the problem of the lustful flesh. Work is God's answer for the problem of play. If Adam had not had to work, he would have used all of his spare time for evil, but through work, God led him on a path of sobriety. Now that our society has invented so many technologies, we do not need to work very much, and this has led us back to the problem of the uncontrolled and overfed lustful flesh.

Recently I observed this as it relates to cards. I sometimes play online solitaire if I get bored. I started playing with a real deck and I found that after a while I got tired of it and quit. Even that small amount of "work" involved in re-dealing the deck is enough to produce the desire to want to do something else. In the virtual world there is never any work, so you never get tired. You just stay glued.

Jesus says, "If any man come after me, he must deny himself." (Matt 16:34). For many of us, dealing with lust means dealing with this more fundamental problem of living a lazy and indulgent lifestyle. Nothing could possibly be lazier than clicking a link and having pleasure come to you. If you want to make progress, you need to begin to embrace a lifestyle of work instead of a lifestyle of indulgence and ease. Do not expect to get free if you do not address this fundamental issue. As Proverbs 21:25 says, "the desire of the sluggard puts him to death." Living a lifestyle based around doing what is easy and getting what you desire leads to destruction. Stop living a life of doing what is easy and a bit at a time embrace a life of work and challenge.

## SOBER SEXUALITY

Part of the reason why sex becomes so addictive to us, is that we allow ourselves to descend into fantasy world that does not reflect real women or real sexuality. We spend hours, days or weeks, chasing a high, obsessing over a certain girl, and the fantasy replaces reality. In this fantasy world, we imagine the woman craving sex just as badly as we do, but that's not reality. It's a fantasy. And when it is reality, it's not a reality you want to live in.

The fact is that God designed you to want sex much more than a woman. It's a physical reality, not simply a psychological one. You have chemicals in your body that make you ready to go. Hers are far more sedate. They make her want to cuddle. Contemporary culture has tried to pretend this is not the case, but you can't wish away biology. And while it is the case, that there are women who love to have a lot of sex, that's not for physical reasons, it's for psychological reasons. These women can be exciting to date, but are a disaster to marry, because she will be looking for sex with the next man, just like you have been looking for it with the next woman.

What men are paying for when they go to sex workers, is not just physical pleasure – that can be had without a woman – what they are paying for is the illusion of being wanted. Erotic dancers dance to make it seem like they are interested in sex, and in particular, interested in sex with you. Prostitutes act like they are interested in sex: for money. They are paid to create that illusion. Most of them are in very broken life situations and have to deal with a lot of borderline repulsive men to make ends meet. It's not a happy life.

When you marry a normal woman, what you find after the honeymoon is over is that there is a significant imbalance in desire between the two of you. It can be frustrating, but it's by design. Instead, she seeks relationship from you which forces you into developing connection – something most men wouldn't do if they didn't have to. Instead of a fantasy life in an imaginary world where your wife craves sex all the time and wants to engage in porn-style fantasies, you need to start to build a healthy sex life together where both of you are trying to connect to one another through sex. The God-given purpose of sex is to bond to your spouse, which is why it's so bad when you do it outside of marriage: you bond to something or someone else and leave your spouse out in the cold.

Neither one of you needs more excitement in the bedroom, what you both need is to learn to develop a regular, healthy, life in the bedroom which addresses your physical needs, and connects you as a couple. As you journey down the path of relationship, you will find that although you may not naturally desire snuggling or chatting, it fulfills deep needs you are not conscious of. It makes you feel connected and therefore reduces your desire to seek artificial connection through a fantasy.

## DISCIPLINE

To live sober, you're going to need self-discipline. I know that sounds rather basic, but it is important to say so, because contemporary American culture, including the church, rejects the idea that discipline could be important to anything. We embrace solutions that say, "If you just do this..." or "If you just believe that... it's so easy." I could sell a million copies if I wrote a book telling you that all you have to do to be free of lust is just believe. It's simple, it's spiritual, and it's misleading.

Any solution you try is going to take work. Even the ones that promise that you don't have to work, will then proceed to tell you what to do. You need to embrace the fact that this is going to take work, and the first part of it is, "Just say no." You cannot defeat lust without discipline. Even if you are walking tightly with God, there are going to be times when you are weak, and in those times you need discipline.

In addition, sin works by a cycle: the more you have, the more you want. I quit eating processed sugar for about a year. It was very difficult. I had intense withdrawals, and my body wanted to get sugar any way I could. I thought for a while that eating without sugar was like a life not worth living. I was depressed. I started eating lots of bland foods. Eventually though, I started to appreciate the natural taste of these foods, which before I thought were boring and uninteresting.

The result was that because I quit eating the fake stuff, I started to enjoy the real stuff. I started to like the flavor of unsweet tea, which I always found way too bitter. I thought that unflavored grits with a little salt tasted like candy. I started snacking on strawberries. My palate changed because I cut out the bad stuff.

You can see where I'm going with this. Looking at porn is a lot like eating processed sugar: it feeds a desire for something unnatural. Every time you look at porn, or think lustful thoughts about a woman, you are feeding the desire, not eliminating it. Sure you feel temporary relief when you masturbate, but you just rewired your brain to associate pleasure with whatever it was you just fantasized about. And the more you feed it, the worse it gets. The less you feed it, the more natural your desires will become. As you start to put more and more distance between yourself and sin, you will notice your desire recalibrating. Things that you once indulged in will seem disgusting. You will slowly begin to look at women as people again, not as potential porn.

To quit sugar, I had to go through serious withdrawals and pain, but eventually the craving for artificial sugar was greatly reduced, and I was able to enjoy healthy foods. It will take discipline to starve yourself out of the way you have wired your brain, but the first step in all of this is to turn off the tap. You are not going to make any progress as long as you are feeding the beast.

And porn is much stronger drug than sugar. Remember, that's what you're dealing with: a drug addiction. When you think lustful thoughts, your brain gets a heavy dose of dopamine, the pleasure chemical in your body. It's that hit of dopamine that you are seeking when you look at porn, or fantasize. You have to slowly rewire your brain, and that only happens if you quit giving yourself the drug in the first place.

In other words, while inner transformation is a critical part of freedom, outward change is the first step. Until you cut off the source, you aren't going to make much progress. And porn is the super-drug – it is always available, anytime, and you can take as much as you need to get the high you want  You will take more and more to get the high you are seeking, all the time increasing the addiction, and further perverting your view of the world, and of women in particular.

When you stop taking the drug, you will of course have intense withdrawals, but you will start the process of rewiring and detoxing your brain. A lot of people get discouraged thinking they are just "white knuckling" their inner addiction, that it is a hopeless battle, and therefore all of the focus should be inward. This is not true. The process of self-denial through discipline works together with inner transformation. Stopping the outward behavior is like stopping pouring gasoline on a fire – it won't put it out, but it will certainly help get the blaze under control.

You need to embrace the fact that this entire process is not going to be easy. Begin to think of yourself more like a SEAL in military training, who must learn to be tough, grit his teeth, and do the right thing even when it is hard. No excuses, no retreat, no surrender. Perhaps you've never done anything hard in your life. If so, that is a kind of problem before the problem. You may have to overhaul your personality to develop that kind of inner strength, but that's what it is going to take to get out of the pit and get to freedom. Maintaining your iron core once you build it is not as hard breaking the inertia and cycle of weakness. And just like any good training, you will need others to push you even as you push yourself.

## Application Questions

1. Think over how you were raised. Were you indulged, as a child or teenager? Did you participate in the party culture?

2. Do you have realistic expectations about women and sex or are you living in a fantasy land? What would you do differently if you recognized the bonding purpose of sex?

3. What can you do to embrace a lifestyle of hard work? What discipline can you introduce into your life?

# "Filters Won't Help"

Lust has been a problem since the very beginning of time, but one thing has changed radically in our generation: access. If your grandfather wanted to avoid pornography and other temptations, all he had to do was stay out of the wrong part of town, and away from the wrong kinds of people, much like if he were trying to avoid drugs. Today, however, most of the people on the planet are about 5 seconds away from watching literally anything they could possibly fantasize about, all served up and produced by a massive global industry. This is not to mention all of the secret temptations offered by the internet involving real people. You don't have to go looking for sex anymore, *it's looking for you*.

What this means is that one important part of freedom is reducing your access. My dad was in security, and one of the things he used to say was that you can never make your house safe, but you can make it a harder target. The same is true with anything you do related to access to pornography. You cannot make it absolutely impossible to view pornography, but you can make harder. And if you are trying to do the right thing, that extra bit of difficulty can make a big difference.

When porn is literally always at your fingertips, it's like an alcoholic always having a bottle on his desk. The temptation will be just too high; any moment of weakness, and he is going to take a drink. Don't fool yourself that you don't need some protection. If you didn't, you wouldn't be reading this book. Honestly, you're not really serious until you're ready to deal with the access issue.

If you are just starting out there is a good chance that you have very strong habits associated with your phone or computer  Just getting around them can be enough to make you want porn.  If that is the case, you need to do whatever it takes to cut off the temptation.  If you have to get radical and go without a smart phone or computer for a while, then do it.  It won't be forever, just until you can get some sobriety.

You can't prevent any possibility of accessing porn anywhere, but you should be able to make it harder and be able to make your home pretty safe at least.  If you can block things at a router level in your house, that's a great idea.  That way any device you use at home is secure.

For security based approaches to work you really need to go the whole way and give the password to someone else so you don't know it.  Make it hard on yourself to cheat.  A drug addict will steal and sell anything he can get his hands on, to pay for the next hit.  You are trying to protect yourself from an addict – it's just that the addict happens to be you.  When an addict goes looking for a fix, they will do whatever is needed to get the fix.  That's generally how you will behave when you are in a moment of weakness, so prepare for it.  You are in your right mind right now, so the normal you needs to plan ahead to protect yourself from the addict in you.  If you really want to go the full distance, talk your system through with another man who can poke holes in it.

My personal favorite is accountability software that will notify someone else when you look at porn.  That way I'm not playing a game of security between myself and a computer, but my integrity to a real person is involved.    It produces the psychology of having someone looking over your shoulder when you are surfing the internet, which honestly, God is all the time. As you get used to "surfing with someone looking over your shoulder" it is a kind of training that makes it normal to use the internet for proper purposes regardless of what filters are or are not in place. Sin flourishes in private, but the light of publicity causes it to dissipate. Getting used to having someone looking over your shoulder, helps you get used to being in public instead of having a private fantasy world where you can escape to sin. Having someone look over your shoulder, starts the process of training yourself to be responsible with freedom, which up until now, you have not been.

Security is not all about filters, however. Consider the basic physical access to your device. Late at night can be a time of extra high risk. Therefore, I do not bring my computer to bed or use my phone at night. Once I start to get tired, it goes off and has to go out of reach. That extra layer of difficulty and the intentionality of doing it makes me much safer. Whereas, if I sit around playing with my phone in bed long enough and late enough, the likelihood of being tempted is very high.

Some people have taken the notion of access to the extreme, as if access were the problem itself. But just like in security, access is not the problem, the burglar is the problem. Access is one of the tools you need to need to use to protect yourself, but it's only a tool. Ultimately you cannot prevent yourself from getting access to anything anywhere for the rest of your life. I met one guy who shut all of his home access down and then went and used porn in the library – a much riskier activity. Blocking access is meant to give you a fighting chance of doing the right thing but it can't stop you. Restricting access is really about retraining yourself to manage freedom, so you can sit down at the library and think about books, not your chance to look at porn.

Eventually you can work your way back down the ladder of accountability. If you got rid of your phone, then set the goal of being able to trust yourself with a phone. If you put complex filters on your devices, then eventually you should be able to get to where accountability is enough.

The Bible compares lust to a fire (1 Cor 7:9). If lust is like a fire, pornography is gasoline. Make it harder to get to the gasoline so you don't start an explosion that will burn your house down.

## Application Questions

1. What is your current level of access? Do you have filters or other accountability systems? If not, why not?

2. What device and situation are the biggest problem for you? What can you change right away to make it harder to be tempted?

3. How can you get someone else involved in your security measures, so that success does not ride only on your own will power?

# "I Can Do It Alone"

## Humble Yourself

Perhaps the hardest part about getting free from sexual addiction is admitting it. Of course that is true with every addiction, but sexual addiction has a greater degree of shame associated with it. Sexual things are embarrassing even to talk about, much less admit that you are "that guy." I remember in college a friend approached me and shared that he was trying to overcome masturbation. The conversation was embarrassing for *me* and I wasn't even the one confessing it. Masturbation is just a very embarrassing activity. Most men don't want to share anything that makes them look weak, much less something so private that makes them look weak. It's a huge barrier to cross. But if you want to be free, it is a very important barrier for you to cross.

The first couple of steps you need to take to get free are going to require you to humble yourself. I know because I lived it and I hated it. Maybe it's easier for some other men, but for me it felt like jumping out of an airplane or cutting my own throat. Now I realize that that was one of the problems behind the problem. If I hadn't been prideful or ashamed, I might have been able to get more significant help when I was younger.

There is a bright side: the Bible says that God shows favor to the humble (Proverbs 3:34). I have found this to be experientially true, and that has changed the way I see the situation. The jump itself has gotten a bit easier as I have gotten used to admitting my embarrassing weaknesses to other men. But I also know there is a reward on the other end – when I go through all of that, God sees it and shows me favor in my life. Not only that, but at a personal level, He knows it's difficult for me and He is with me in it. Are you ready to get humble and get free?

## WHY YOU NEED ACCOUNTABILITY

One popular book on sexual sin basically dismisses the role of accountability in the freedom process, but my experience has taught me otherwise. Accountability is a very helpful part of the freedom process, as long as it is the right kind.

I spent some of my formative years in a very controlling Christian group. In this group you were supposed to bare all to a mentor, but I felt rejected and judged by this group of people more generally. This made it very difficult for me to want to have any kind of accountability with them. Confessing a major weakness was an invitation to be looked down upon and judged even more. I was pretty sure any stories would leak upwards to the leadership, causing more judgment. Long after I left this group, I was terrified of getting anyone else very closely involved in my struggle for purity. Accountability was anything but helpful or safe.

The other thing that can make accountability difficult is trying to make it work with someone who has never really struggled with lust—with one of those "normal" guys that I said this book isn't for. Someone like that simply isn't going to understand why this is so difficult for you and why you can't just "fix it." Even if they are loving and understanding, you may find yourself in a performance trap of always trying to be as good as they are. Opening up repeatedly to a person like that will probably make you very discouraged.

Other people who promote accountability think that shame is what it is all about – if confessing is shameful and hard enough then it will deter you from doing it. It may deter you for a while, but eventually you will just become extremely stressed out. Then you will act out anyway or cheat the system. Good accountability is not about being psychologically stressed, it's about being transparent and taking responsibility for yourself.

No one else other than me will stand before God and give account for my life. You don't report to an accountability group to see if they will accept or forgive you. You report to a group to challenge yourself to do the right thing, and to be honest to yourself when you're not living right. I have to raise the bar on myself, and keep my own conscience clean before God. A good accountability partner or group does not take initiative away from you or put pressure on you, but helps you challenge yourself to do your best. It should be more like a spotter in a gym and less like a confessor in a booth. I want to "beat my own times," be the best I can be, and be brutally honest with myself about where I am. Good accountability is a system which triggers this to happen on a regular basis. It keeps me in the race when I feel like jumping the track.

Of course, accountability does introduce the possibility of correction or confrontation, but remember, "Faithful are the wounds of a friend; but the kisses of an enemy are deceitful." (Prov. 27:6). I have been confronted a few times, and it stung, but it the fact is that being corrected on earth by a friend is vastly superior to the eternal consequences that come from staying in sin.

Getting comfortable being corrected was especially difficult for me. I am a very sensitive person, and I did not receive a lot of correction growing up. Yet, the walk of freedom is going to involve people telling you things that are uncomfortable. Over time I came to learn that getting all emotional in response to correction was just another symptom of the problem. Part of being a man is doing what is difficult and taking it straight from other men, without melting down.

I'm not talking about someone being abusively rude. I'm talking about when friends tell you the truth, like a coach of a team or a sergeant in the army. They are telling you what you need to hear for your own good. It's not the end of the world, it's just the truth. The truth can hurt, but rather than get hurt, I learned to just take action to fix it. It took me quite a long time to get to this place, but as I started down the path, I found that in addition to steering me down the right path, it ministered a missing piece of manliness to my life. Taking it on the chin can be hard, but you can do it, after all, you're a man.

## GROUP ACCOUNTABILITY

This is what I believe the genius of Alcoholics Anonymous and other similar groups is: you are not confessing to a bunch of people who think they have it all together, you are confessing to a bunch of people who realize they have a similar problem. This makes all the difference in how they treat you and how it feels to you as a participant.

I have also learned that making a good friend your accountability partner, even someone who has struggled, can put pressure on the relationship. Your friendship can turn into a confession booth. If you are in ministry, you have a moral responsibility to make sure that those you minister with know how you are doing, but I do not recommend your closest associates playing the role of ongoing accountability partner or coach. It's better to have someone outside your immediate situation who is specifically there to help you on your journey.

This is where the "anonymous" part of AA becomes important. While my good friends know how I'm doing in general, and I have given them permission to ask me for details anytime they want them, they are not the ones I am reaching out to with all of the details on a regular basis. Finding a good group that deals with sexual addiction is better for that, especially if the members are relatively anonymous to you.

While I resisted this for years, I now highly recommend anyone who is really struggling to join a group. You will meet other people who are struggling with you, and you will be able to encourage each other and challenge each other to get to the next level. Most importantly, it will help you start to form a new life habit. Each week requires you to be completely honest with others about how you are doing, and that will progressively lead you to not want to have anything to report. It forms the psychological habit of purity. This is the habit that other men have that you need.

Time should not be an issue. There are many groups which meet in secular places or churches throughout the week. There are even online groups that you can join. I find some poetic justice in this. Pornography is a problem created by the internet, and now internet-based groups can be part of the solution. You participate in these groups by joining a conference call once a week at a regular time.

## GETTING OVER THE HURDLE
The thought of joining a group can be extremely negative, especially for a man, because it is an admission of being weak and having a problem. Additionally, it can be embarrassing to tell a bunch of other men your sexual

struggles. But this is now one of the first things I recommend when someone approaches me with an issue because once you get over that hump, you are going to find a group of people that can really help you move along, keep you focused, and keep it positive. That doesn't mean that a group is all peaches and cream – your friends in the group may challenge you—but you will know that you're in it together, and that makes all the difference in the world.

At first joining a group may make you feel like your life revolves around being "an addict," but that's a trap that you will get past with a little time. Instead of thinking all week about the issue at any random time, you know there will be a focused time when you have to deal with it. Addict for an hour, normal for a week. Over time, I've come to find it is like keeping my car tuned up. Being honest once a week with a group forces me to be honest with myself about whether I am on the right path or not. Doing a weekly tune-up keeps me from a breakdown that will get me stranded on the side of the road.

There are reasons why groups have been used for the past hundred years as the primary and most important tool in recovery from alcohol addiction: they work. They provide a unique set of dynamics which can really help you because:

- Members understand the struggle personally, so they will be merciful but also will not be fooled by a smokescreen.

- There's a healthy "competition" where you do not want to let the team down and where you strive to do as well as the others.

- They provide an open setting where you are committed and able to tell the whole truth. The leaders have heard it all before.

- It spreads accountability over multiple different relationships, so no-one person or relationship is overburdened with your issue.

None of this means you have to check in forever. The group is just a tool in helping you get to where you need to be. For me, and for many others, these additional factors have made the difference between going up or going down, and having a consistent pattern of success instead of victory for just a season.

### WIVES

One question that often comes up for married men is, "What role does my wife play in accountability?" First of all, she does need to know what you are going through. You have a moral obligation to tell your wife when you are having trouble because you have made a covenant before God to love her and forsake all others. If you are acting out sexually, you aren't doing that.

This can be very hard for wives, especially the first time you confess. Some take it better than others, but all women will feel insecure, unloved, and many other similar kinds of feelings. For this reason, I recommend that you and your wife agree that you are going to get help from an accountability group, and that you will keep her aware of how you are doing overall, but you will not involve her in the "blow by blow." It places too much pressure on her to be worried all of the time what you might be thinking. Most wives will be ok with this when they know you are getting help and being completely transparent with someone else. I keep no secrets from my wife, and so I will tell her anything she wants to know at any time, but we don't go over the details unless she asks.

As a woman, and in particular as one who needs your affections, your wife is not well-positioned to be your sexual accountability partner. But she is well positioned to play a different and even more important role: She is your *life* accountability partner. She lives with you all of the time. She may know things are shaky with you even before you do. Perhaps your situation started because you never developed the capacity for real emotional intimacy with your wife, and you turned to porn and fantasies as a substitute.

Begin to build a relationship with your wife where she is the counselor and friend in the deeper heart issues of your life, especially whatever you need to work through to be free. Most women are thrilled when their husband wants to open up. Learn how to open up to her and share your weaknesses. Begin the journey of talking to her about the things that are hard to tell another man, such as your fears, loneliness, and disconnection from others. If the two of you have trouble having good heart-to-heart conversations, then start working on your marriage with another couple so that the two of you can learn to communicate.

In addition, start to build healthy routines of connection together. Your wife is part your daily life and so you should make that fact work for you. Being in healthy routines together is a strong defense against sin. I have found that even if I don't think I'm getting anything in particular out of going out together, I actually am, residually. The simple habit of going to bed together every night, and starting off snuggling with her is a powerful connection point that operates on the subconscious level. Together, the two of us practice staying connected at all phases of the day, and especially before bed. As we have worked to build that connection we have both discovered many things we do which lead to disconnection and have had to adapt in order to build that strong connection. Porn is a relationship killer, but relationship is a porn killer.

You should develop good habits of being together, going to sleep together, and other ways that help ground you in real life instead of a fantasy life. If you are married and escaping to porn, it doesn't mean you don't love your wife, but it does mean that the two of you are not as bonded as you should be. Building a lifestyle of transparency and togetherness is the best kind of accountability you can have and your wife will love you for it.

Remember, accountability is a tool, not a magic solution. Sometimes you can get around people who think that more accountability is always better, but I think that's also a trap. What happens is, you start to feel good about yourself for all the accountability partners you have, or you feel bad for not having enough. I've known guys with multiple layers of accountability and structure who aren't really making any progress. They're just getting more frustrated as they confess to five different people every time they fall. What you need are relationships that help you stay open and honest on a consistent basis, in the key areas where you struggle. You can have more than one, if each plays a certain role. Make those relationships work for you on the path to freedom.

## Application Questions

1. Do you have trouble opening up to others? How has it gone when you have admitted weakness to others?

2. Do you have trouble receiving correction? How would you behave differently if you "took it like a man"?

3. Who around you would make good accountability partners and what role could they play? List options for online and local groups.

4. How could you improve your relationship with your wife? List some habits you could develop together and areas you could discuss.

# "I Can Play With Fire"

One of the reasons why sexual temptation has become such a major issue for men who want to do the right thing is because our society is saturated in sex. We've all heard this comment many times, but what does it actually mean? What can you practically do about it?

When I was in college, I went to a Dave Matthews Band concert because I thought they had great music. I was shocked to find that the concert was full of college aged girls who were responding sexually to the music. Looking back, the only thing surprising about this is that I found it surprising. Listening closely to the words of many Dave Matthews songs, and for that matter most rock songs, they are literally filled with sexually suggestive material.

Somehow we think we can fill ourselves with these kinds of things and not be affected. You think that because a song doesn't cause you to think or feel sexual in the moment, that it isn't affecting you, but that is wrong. In reality, the song is part of what subconsciously forms your worldview toward life and toward women. Some would go as far as to say that there is a spiritual component: that when you listen to music, you are participating in an act of worship—either the worship of God, or the worship of sin, just like the Israelites did around the Golden Calf.

Consequently, one of the steps of freedom is cutting this kind of garbage out and replacing it with God-centered worship music. Honestly, if you're a committed Christian you should have done that anyway, but just in case you need an extra push, realize that it is feeding the dragon you are trying to kill.

The same is true for movies and television. A great deal of television and movies have heavy sexual themes in an otherwise interesting plot. You have to cut these things out. You will become what you behold. You can't clean your house if you have a sewer running into it.

## THE BIG CHALLENGE

Cleaning up your media diet is a required first step, but in my opinion, media is not really the main way society is sexually saturated. In my opinion, perhaps the greatest danger is the most seemingly innocuous of all: girls.

For most of history women and men were raised and educated separately. It was only in the 20th century that we started putting them together. I can say about my own education, that I remember more about the girls I was interested in growing up than any single subject I studied. That's what I thought about on the way to school, when I was getting dressed in the morning, when I got out of classes, and when free time came afterwards. What girl did I like, how could I get her attention, and when I had one, what were we going to do together. I'm not saying I never thought about anything else, I'm just saying that when you put adolescent girls and boys together, a large majority of them are going to spend a large majority of their time thinking about each other.

Not only that, but the girls around you are near the peak of their attractiveness and they are trying to get the attention of boys (even if you are not one of them). Therefore, you are not just around a lot of girls. You are around attractive girls who are looking for attention. It's crazy that we would put kids in this situation and expect them not to come out sex addicted. Even if nothing sexual happens, you're still immersed in a sexually charged environment.

As an adult, I make a similar observation. Over the course of my career, I have had to work with many women, and for the most part temptation has not been a major issue at the workplace. The reason is because most of the women I have worked with are not looking for sexual attention from me or anyone else. They are usually married moms who are thinking about work and kids. They aren't sending signals that they want attention.

However, being around a single woman, or a woman who is starved in her marriage can be quite a different story. When a woman wants attention it subconsciously cues you to give attention, and that leads you down the path to temptation. Even if you are completely honorable with her in person, it will start the engine of sexuality and may lead you into temptation later that night when you are alone or even days later, until you get it out of your head.

If as a married man you ever find yourself in a situation where a woman is intentionally giving you attention, *run, don't walk.* Women are subconsciously trained from their teen years how to reject attention from men that they don't want attention from, and get it from those who they do, but the average man, on the other hand, is very vulnerable to these cues, especially if they're coming from an attractive woman.

I once found myself in a compromising position with a woman in a professional situation because I told her she had "executive potential." While I meant this as a professional complement, for her it struck a chord, probably because she felt undervalued in that area. After that, she turned on the charm. Before I knew what was going on, I was returning her attention and eventually had to cut her off completely and repent before it turned into something more. I have since learned to be more careful about what I say to a woman, and to intentionally send distancing messages if I feel interest coming from her.

Most of this process is really about you getting victory over yourself, but make no mistake, there is a devil and at times he will set traps for you to fall into. He does not want you just walking out to freedom. A trap is a situation that plays to your specific weaknesses and that you didn't bring on yourself directly. It's like when I was on a long trip in a hotel room and out of nowhere a woman nearby who had no way of knowing I was in her city messaged me and started showing interest. It was at a particularly weak time too. All I would have needed to do is show her a little interest, and I could have ruined everything in a blink of an eye. It was a trap. The thing about a trap is that you think you can get the bait and walk out, but like an animal reaching for the bait, the trap is set to lead you to destruction.

I had been walking into these kinds of traps over and over again until one day a friend gave me Proverbs 22:3: *"The wise man sees danger and hides himself, but the fool goes on and suffers for it.."* Suddenly I realized what a fool I had been. When I sensed a trap, I would poke at the bait until I got in over my head. Now I've learned my lesson, as soon as I realize I'm in a setup, I run. I want to be the fox that lives to my next meal, not the one that becomes the next meal. When your old High School girlfriend suddenly wants to hang out, or the your professional colleague wants to go out for a drink, don't take the bait. Be smart and walk away.

## SUMMARY

In summary, the primary and most powerful way you will experience the sex saturation of culture is not on a billboard or a magazine, or even a TV show, it is in the women you have contact with or see in public. Perhaps this is one of the reasons why most societies throughout history placed women in family context until they were married off, usually at a young age. Placing single men around single women for extended periods is sexualizing for everyone involved. Placing married men and women together is safer, but not always.

When a woman is looking for attention, even if it is not from you, it has a very powerful effect on your mind. Most men are not aware of the fact that "sexy" women have to put a lot of work into it; they aren't just born that way. In additional to natural beauty, they must put a lot of effort into creating a sexy image: in her hair, her clothes, her jewelry, her makeup, her scent, her mannerisms, and in the way she talks. She has carefully crafted this image because she wants attention from someone. When you are exposed to those signals, you are wired to respond by giving her that attention.

I have personally found this to be an empowering revelation. I close my heart to feeding the attention needs of any woman who is proactively seeking it in any sexual or flirty way, whether that is a look, a conversation or a thought. This is what Proverbs 5 has in mind when it says:

> For the lips of the adulterous woman drip honey,
>> and her speech is smoother than oil;
> But in the end she is bitter as gall,
>> sharp as a double-edged sword.
> Her feet go down to death;
>> Her steps lead straight to the grave.

She gives no thought to the way of life;

> Her paths wander aimlessly, but she does not know it.

To really understand this passage, you have to realize it's not just talking about a married woman who is looking for an affair. It is speaking about any woman who is seeking that kind of attention from a man whom she is not married to (or considering marriage with). According to the Bible, she may not even know what she is doing, but it's deadly to both people, nonetheless.

What advice does the Bible give to us when we encounter a woman matching this profile? "Keep to a path far from her, do not go near the door of her house." Or simply: **stay away**. Going to the door of her house is the last step, but by the time your mind is there, you're almost cooked. When you recognize this kind of woman, do not feed on it either in your mind, with your gaze or with your personal attention. If you pay attention to her, you're in the trap.

Sometimes I wonder if that is what happened to Joseph with Potiphar's wife. She clearly wanted attention from him. Maybe he got just a little bit too friendly with her, and then she moved in on him. By the time he disengaged, he spared himself from sin, but he was already in trouble, and found himself in a dungeon.

They key in all of this is developing a sober worldview about women. Women are human beings with needs that are very similar to your own. Most women need love and security much more than they need sex, but some are willing to trade one for the other.

## Application Questions

1. Is your media diet clean? Think about the music you listen to, and the movies and TV you watch. Do they include sexual themes?

2. If you are married, do you have any relationships where you are giving too much attention to a woman?

3. Think back over times when you have had major falls. Did you step into a trap? What can you look for to avoid being trapped again?

# "I'm Not Vulnerable"

As you begin to get some victories, you will start to encounter the deception of success. You will find that you are going along quite well for a while and then suddenly, as if out of nowhere, you fall. One of the reasons for this is because there are moments of vulnerability which can creep up on you with you noticing.

In addiction recovery, the acronym HALT, standing for Hungry, Angry, Lonely, Tired, is often used to describe when someone is most vulnerable to temptation, and I think it is contains a lot of hidden wisdom. For Christians dealing with lust, my experience is that the lonely and tired are the most important of those. In fact, of all of the things I've done over the years to deal with temptation, prioritizing going to sleep may be the single most important.

When you are tired, your inhibitions get worn down. You experience a state somewhat like being drunk. In fact, I would go as far as to say that the subconscious reason why we stay up is to experience that state of emotional relaxation, and perhaps the porn that goes with it. In this late night state it is much easier to be tempted, and perhaps even an inevitability.

If you stay up late enough, and you are on the computer, you are almost certain to be in trouble. I now take going to sleep and staying rested very seriously, like it was the sin itself. I try to make it a point to go to bed when my wife goes to bed, and to keep the computer out of reach. And the red line is this: the first time I feel tempted late at night, I know I have stayed up too late and it is time for me to roll over and go to bed. I can't tell you how much that has helped me personally, and I know from other men that night time is often the same kind of challenge. A solid bed routine is a great defense against temptation.

Some guys want to go to sleep, but have a very hard time when they are being tempted, and that adds a whole additional layer. Caffeine is one thing to consider. If you look on the web, it is commonly believed that caffeine leaves your system in 3-6 hours, but I can attest that this is not the case. It takes more like 1-3 days to totally get out. Just stop drinking all caffeine for a couple of days and see how tired you are. Your body will not act normal until several days later. Therefore, if going to bed is difficult for you, I would challenge you to cut caffeine out of your diet completely, until you are able to sleep. And then if you add it back in, do so carefully. Personally, I just went to decaf permanently. Sugar can also affect your ability to sleep. You may need to reduce that as well, especially late at night.

In addition, in the early going, on the really hard days, I would do pushups until I could barely move to help me get tired enough to sleep, and on the most extreme days, take some kind of sleep aid. You can see where I'm going with this. I started taking going to sleep as a major battle in the war for freedom, not just a side issue. It wasn't too long after adopting this mindset that it got a lot easier and started to become a non-factor. If you can avoid being up when you shouldn't be, you will avoid a world of difficulty.

The same can be said about being lonely. Guys who travel a lot, like I do, often have trouble in their hotel rooms. Hotel rooms can be a very lonely and boxed in place. I used to experience a lot of temptation when going to hotel rooms until I created certain habits:

- I never turn the TV on. It is as if the TV was not even there. This keeps me from being in a situation where I am looking to the TV to meet my needs, which inevitably leads to looking for something titillating.

- I start working in the room as soon as I get set up. This turns my hotel room into another office rather than a lonely place. I do emails and other projects and the time goes quickly.

- I try to call or video-call home to stay connected with my family or friends.

I can say now that hotel rooms do not generally present very much temptation for me because I've made these decisions. I feel more like I'm working from my home office than a dark lonely place. And just as importantly as all of these, I try to limit my travel to a manageable level. Travel breaks your cycles and strains the emotional bonds that keep you safe. Long and extensive travel can place a huge burden on you.

As far as being "angry," I would generalize that to "stress." If you have unresolved negative emotions, you are more likely to turn to pornography or sexual sin. Many men are simply unable to access their emotions, and pornography is a way to get an emotional release. If you fit this pattern, you need to seek help specific to the problem you are dealing with, whether it is depression, anger, self-loathing or some other major issue, all of these things will drive you to sexual sin for the high that takes them away. If you are under stress, recognize that you are potentially vulnerable and do things to bring your stress level down before your stress issue becomes a sin issue.

Sometimes traditional models of addiction take this point too far, and try to connect all addiction with unresolved issues like stress or loneliness, and I simply do not believe that is the case with sexual sin. Sexual sin is addictive no matter how you are feeling because it's a high. Still, a high is much more attractive when you are having a deep low. If you have a lot of negativity you need to deal with that before you're going to make much progress. You need to recognize that when you are physically or emotionally worn down, temptation is right around the corner, and so you should not allow yourself to be taken by surprise, by changing your habits, you can close these doors.

### YOUR ENERGY LEVEL

One of the things I have learned along the course of life is that some activities require a lot of emotional and spiritual energy, and some require very little. For me to write this booklet, for example, takes a very high level of spiritual energy. I have to focus, think, and bring forth ideas from inside myself. On the other end of the spectrum are things like playing computer solitaire or watching a TV show. These require a very low level of energy. And there are many things in the middle, like fixing things around the house, spending time with other people, playing an instrument, reading a book, calling a friend, even getting food.

One of the religious traps that the devil creates is to make everything except reading your Bible or praying (which require a lot of spiritual energy) a sin, and therefore leave you with nothing legitimate to do when you have low energy and are vulnerable.

In a lot of cases, this low energy simply needs I need to go to sleep. Funny thing is, I didn't know to do that before. Between caffeine, testosterone, and our driven way of thinking of life, men can really struggle with wanting to go to sleep. Once I started paying attention to my level of spiritual energy, I started to realize when I was tempted even if I didn't "feel tired" and would just go to sleep.

But if you are not tired enough for sleep, then you need something to do in those times when you can't do much that is productive. But sometimes our religious training might lead us to do just the opposite. Since you are trying to be "holy" by living free from lust, you feel obligated to do something even more holy when you are tempted. In the early phases of freedom especially, you need to just stay focused on not sinning. The Holy thing you are doing right now is cutting sin out of your life. You don't need to add to it by fasting, praying and doing all kinds of religious duties. It is sufficient right now that you are turning your life away from sin and addiction.

So don't feel bad if you have to use some transitional activities at first to help you in these times. I used my favorite solitaire game and documentaries, and TV to help me at first. Many men watch sports. Then I graduated to doing more productive things, such as calling friends or spending time with family as much as I could. These kinds of low spiritual energy activities give me a chance to reset myself without provoking sin, and I consider them to be a key part of the healthy lifestyle that helps keep me out of the danger zone. Ideally, your escape activity should be as wholesome as possible, but remember that anything better than sexual sin is a good option.

## Application Questions

1.  Do stress or unexpressed emotion drive you to act out? If so, what healthy ways can you deal with your stress?

2.  Does loneliness play an important part in your temptation? If so, what you do to be more connected?

3.  Do you have trouble going to sleep, and does temptation increase when you do? If so, what can you do to change your sleep habits?

4.  What escape activities can you do when you are feeling tempted? Make a list of several low-energy options.

# "Women Are For Pleasure"

## Getting to the Root of the Problem

Lust is not an isolated issue. It is deeply integrated into who you are in many ways. A lot of guys say, "If I just didn't struggle with this, everything else in my life would be great." But that is based on a false idea of what you are struggling with. First of all, lust is often a fruit just as much as it is a root. Pretty much any problem a man has is likely to manifest itself through lust. Are you depressed? Nothing a little masturbation won't fix. Girl trouble? Nothing a little porn fantasy can't fix. Bad week on the job? Why not have a chat with a cam girl who will make you forget about it? Men are often not very aware of our emotions, and therefore sexual sin becomes the "one size fits all" solution to every kind of life problem.

Secondly, for those with a stronghold, lust is deeply rooted into your personality. It's not just a little add-on issue that you can fix and then everything is great. It requires an overhaul of your identity. Therefore, to fight and win this war, you need a comprehensive approach which addresses all of the aspects of life which are leading you down the road to sin. When you look at it this way, it's easier to understand why you have had such a hard time defeating it. It's not just a little problem. It's a comprehensive problem that will touch every aspect of who you are before you're done.

So far we've looked at some of the external factors we need to gain control, but what about the deeper psychological factors? It is important that you start to look at the problem holistically instead of in isolation. If you know, for example, that you have deep problems with confidence, depression, narcissism, trauma, abusive relationships, unforgiveness, etc., then you should start explicitly attacking those problems, understanding that they play a part in a system that leads you to sin. Sexual sin is simply one of the medications you are using to try and deal with the pain from those issues.

## THE NEED TO CONNECT

Everyone human being needs healthy connections to other people. When lust gets involved, this becomes broken either by seeking connection all of the time like a glutton at a feast, or by replacing human connection with virtual connections or self-connection. The social addict is more addicted to the relationship than the sex itself while the antisocial addict uses sex or porn as a substitute for having a relationship. It is not that one is better or worse than the other, it is just helpful to recognize which one you are.

If you are a social addict, women are a greater temptation for you than porn. You might use porn, but it probably because you are trying to avoid getting into sin with live women. You are the kind of person that when put in close contact with any moderately attractive women, you are likely to start to form or feel a connection. You are likely more emotionally aware than the average man, perhaps chatty, and know how to talk to a woman on her level. You are the kind of person who is in great danger of having affairs.

If you are a social addict, you need to learn how to develop healthy boundaries with women. Not just physically healthy boundaries, but emotional ones. You naturally build emotional connections which can lead both you and women into sin. You may not even be consciously aware of it, but you are doing things that send them cues to be close, or encouraging them if they seek you for closeness. You need to stop sending women these signals if you want to stay free. You need to learn how to be more "professional" in the way you relate to women.

This will take some work and practice because if you are a social addict, you are getting a huge thrill from these kinds of interactions. When you take it away, you will likely feel lonely and bored. In our culture we are used to having no social limits on appropriate distance between the sexes, but that's a huge part of the problem. Especially if you're the kind of person who has had more close friendships with women than men over the course of your life, then this step may be very hard for you. It may even seem like legalism because, after all, you've been able to have boundaries with some women. You might not see why becoming old-fashioned about it is part of the answer.

If this is you, you just need to start practicing having appropriate distance. Every man I know that is free does this. Don't fool yourself; you can't dangle candy in your face all day and not eventually want to take a bite. This does not mean in the long run that you can never be friendly with any woman or have a personal conversation. My rule is to be honest with myself about whether a woman is potentially attractive. I am more relaxed with women I am not attracted to in any way. I know the difference and my wife does too. Telling the old lady upstairs your woes is not going to lead either of you into temptation. The more potential for attraction there is on either end, however, the more effort I make to be professional and keep a safe distance.

If you are an antisocial addict, on the other hand, the computer screen is where you seek comfort. The fantasy world of porn is comfortable for you. If you are having real-life sex, it is probably less about the emotional connection to the woman, and more about the ways it makes you feel. The social addict is addicted to the relationship, but you are bent towards *not* having a relationship. Porn and other factors have stunted your natural relational growth. You need to turn off the porn and begin to put yourself in social settings where you learn to value and succeed in real life relationships of all kinds. Find a mentor who can help you break out of your shell so that you will be ready to seek a real life relationship with a potential mate. Or, if you are married, find a group or couple who can help you and your wife move closer to each other without stress or emotional letdown.

## THE FANTASY LIFE

Pornography is a kind of designer fantasy. What you like to watch is tailor-made to satisfy you in just the ways that you most crave. This is part of the power of the addiction, but it's also part of the way out: Real love is when someone cares for you, is with you in difficult times, listens to your concerns, and helps you face the challenges of life together. Real love is much less exciting than pornography, but it's *real*. Part of getting free is when you start to appreciate real love more than the fantasy world created by pornography.

The same kind of fantasy world can be created with real women as well. There is a natural thrill associated with a woman who wants your attention, and wants to be close to you, especially when this person is new to you. This is the source of the so-called "honeymoon" phase of relationships: both people are experiencing the thrill of attention from someone else. The intensity of this excitement frequently clouds people's judgment and leads them to make bad decisions. Real love begins when the thrill is over.

It is also this thrill that leads people into affairs. No matter how amazing your relationship is with someone when you start out, it will eventually become routine for both of you. You become family and develop feelings that are more like family and less like Hollywood. For many, the addiction to thrill is alluring and the first woman who provides the thrill again will open a gateway to an affair.

Some people become deluded by the thrilling feelings into thinking that the new woman is their true "soul mate" or even "spiritual mate," but that's a lie. After a few years, if you divorce your spouse for the new person, you will find yourself in the same place as before and seeking a new thrill. If you do not divorce again, you might use a mistress for the thrill while using your wife for her true love.

## COVERED OR UNCOVERED?

The ultimate step of freedom is when you develop new eyes toward women in general. The problem for you, as someone who has given into addiction, is that you may never have looked at women in a healthy way, or if you have, you have forgotten how.

An addict looks at women from the perspective of how exciting they are. Women exist and are valued based on how much they please you. Women who you do not find attractive are almost like a third gender. You don't even notice them or think of them as women.

A healthy man looks at women not from a perspective of need, but from a perspective of care. You are the protector and caregiver for women—for all women, but especially those in your life. The spiritual term for this attitude is "covering." Your role is to cover women, not to uncover them.

This is the proper relationship between men and women, and it is the one that has been aggressively undermined in contemporary society. Problems in this area are as old as the Garden of Eden, however. Adam's role was to protect and care for his wife, but instead he *followed her* into temptation. When she came out from under his protection, they were both destroyed. The dramatic success of feminism in our culture means that many men under 40 simply have not seen, much less experienced, a healthy relationship where the woman fully relies on a man this way as we did in generations past. This destructive cultural cycle has affected all of us in ways that are so extensive it's hard to really even see them. Our growing societal problems with lust are not simply because we have access to porn or permissive beliefs—they have been completely encoded in the way we relate to one another.

The failure of this protective relationship is directly related to women physically uncovering themselves, either to gain attention or because men pay them to. When a woman uncovers herself, she is tempting you into the upside-down relationship that Adam started in the Garden where a man follows a woman. While many women do this voluntarily for the thrill that it brings to have the attention of men, the end result is always bondage for both.

When you encounter a woman who has uncovered herself, your heart is supposed to reflectively want to cover her, to protect her from sin, from other men, and to show her that her value is not in her appearance but in her identity as a child of God. Her uncovering is not purely physical, but also emotional and spiritual. With certain women or in certain situations, you will be able to feel the pull of a woman's desire for your attention, regardless of how she is dressed.

Have you ever been around a woman who just has "something about her" that is really sexy and provokes desire even though there is nothing particular about her appearance? This comes from her own desire for men to want her. You feel it and allow it draw you in. What you see or don't see is just a physical manifestation of this inner heart condition. Women are not supposed to do this. They are supposed to be chaste in heart and not draw you in like that, but if you sense one who does, realize that it is nothing desirable. It's something you want to get away from.

Some women do these kinds of things to get the attention of a man because they need it. They work hard to attract men and be beautiful they are needy and insecure deep down. Getting attention from enough men will make her feel temporarily full or even overfull, but as soon as the attention is gone, she will feel that need again. When you see this for what it is, it becomes less attractive. When I see a woman and I feel that desire to worship or feed my heart on her beauty, I remind myself that this is an illusion and return my heart to the posture of a protector and caregiver. It's a powerful illusion, but it's still an illusion. Seeing through this illusion is part of working the idolatry out of your heart.

The Bible says that the "woman is the glory of man." (1 Cor. 11:7) This explains why when a woman uncovers herself, men are drawn to her in ways that transcend logic. Your flesh in its fallen state will respond to this by wanting to worship her, and fulfill that worship through sex. You become convinced that she is perfect and that attention from her will satisfy your desires. This is built in to the fallen state of man. Some men think that they can become strong enough not to be tempted, but that's a trap. Being strong means recognizing and walking away from temptation so your flesh does not rule. On the flip side, when a woman who is chaste in heart shows you value and respect, it can have the opposite effect—it can trigger your desire to protect her and respect her back.

As you get far enough along the process of freedom, you will begin to learn to conduct this kind of relationships with women that will actually insulate you from temptation, rather than lead you into it. You can develop a pure heart toward women over time, but it will need to be maintained vigilantly because the structure of our society is that women no longer go covered and protected either emotionally or physically.

## Application Questions

1. Do you have other personal issues which may be feeding into your sexual addiction? What steps can you take to address those?

2. Are you more of a social addict, or an antisocial addict? What can you do to practice healthy relationships with others?

3. Are you able to think of attractive women in your life as a protector rather than as a pleasure source? Conversely, do you show kindness to women you are not attracted to, or do you treat them as if they don't exist?

# "Women Are Better Than Men"

Lust has been a problem in every society at all times, but we can all see how America in the past 100 years has gone from a very conservative and self-controlled culture to one where even highly motivated Christian leaders can barely stop looking at porn. Why is lust out of control in our society? There is something bigger at work than just what is common to individuals. We have a culture problem.

Culture is the invisible web of thoughts and attitudes behind every relationship you have and how you see the world. It is very difficult to think or feel differently than your culture tells you to, because the reinforcements are everywhere. You can vary slightly from cultural norms, but likely you cannot even imagine what it would be and feel like to be from another culture.

To understand how culture works and how powerful it is, consider Haiti, where the culture is based on voodoo—a form of witchcraft. Most Americans and Europeans in general think that voodoo is a dumb superstition. We place no stock in it. Haitians, however, have seen crazy things done through voodoo. They know it is real.

What is amazing is that Haitians have a saying that "Voodoo doesn't work on white people." Because Americans don't see the world in terms of voodoo, it has no power over them. Haitian Christians, however, even though they reject voodoo and turn to Jesus, still have these kinds of thoughts and experiences deep in their minds and are more vulnerable, even though they have access to the power of the Risen Lord. The "voodoo cultural wiring," if you will, is very deep in a Haitian person. It's hard to get out. That is the power of culture. It teaches you how to think and see the world.

This is the kind of thing we're talking about with lust and American culture. There are invisible aspects of our culture that teach us at a young age to lust, and those things then wire us to be addicted to lust as adults. The experiences you've had growing up supercharge your thought processes with lust in ways that you would never have experienced 100 years ago, or if you lived today in some other culture. In other words, you are not just fighting your own personal battle, you are fighting to see the world differently than your entire culture and upbringing have taught you to subconsciously see and feel about it.

## THE VALUE OF MANLINESS

While there are many areas where culture is programming us, the one seriously affecting freedom from lust is the destruction of manliness and the family. This is not a root issue for all men, but it is for many, especially educated men and ones who were raised in a Christian home.

For thousands of years, men were valued and respected as protectors and providers. They were expected to be strong and brave, and this was considered valuable. Women wanted that kind of man, and other men respected that kind of man. Men derived a great deal of worth and satisfaction from this arrangement, and women were attracted to it.

But in the last few decades there has been an assault on manliness. We don't value men for being men anymore. We value a man if he is sensitive, soft, and gentle. And we expect him to defer to a woman in any conflict, personal or professional. It is unacceptable for him to be a real man or the head of the household anymore. Women are promoted as amazing and attractive, and men as unnecessary. In the words of one feminist, "A woman needs a man like a fish needs a bicycle."

What this kind of cultural messaging does is make you crave attention and affection from a woman. It takes away the value you have in yourself and the value that your grandfather would have felt just about being a man. It also puts all of our focus on women. When a woman gives you attention, this gives you self-worth and value, because in our society, women are supposed to have the attention, and men aren't. This is an emasculation problem and increases sexual addiction. What you are getting from porn, sex, and other encounters with women, is acceptance and affirmation.

On top of this, promising women "liberation" actually leads them into stress and bondage. Instead of being able to trust that the men in their life will protect them, most now believe they need to protect themselves. Having to protect yourself makes you tough instead of soft and vulnerable. This places a burden on women which prevents them from loving the men in their lives to the full capacity. So there's a double assault going on in our culture: you've been told to be more womanly, and women have been told to be more manly. Not only do you end up feeling starved, you are starving for something that many women no longer even know how to give.

This creates emasculation and deep emotional needs that are hard to fulfill. If this describes you, then you may have had an "upside-down family" where your mom fulfilled more of the traditional dad role, and your dad was passive, absent, or fulfilled more of the motherly role. This can make you crave real feminine attention and comfort. Some of the common patterns to look for in your history include:

- If your mom was in charge of the house.

- If your father was very quiet or submissive to your mom. If life revolved around your mom more generally.

- If your dad allowed himself to be mocked, or manliness to be made fun of

- If you did not do many competitive or manly activities as a boy.

- If your father doted on the girls, but ignored the boys. Especially so if his attention to the girls had lustful overtones.

- If you grew up thinking that only feminine virtues were desirable.

These are the kinds of things that create emasculation, and it has the effect of supercharging lust. You are always craving a woman because she has what you lack. She is perfect and valuable, but you are just a man.

You need to realize this is all a lie cooked up by hell. God places a very high value on masculine virtues. Jesus doesn't seem very "loving" by a feminine American definition, but He is very loving by a masculine definition. He showed His love by His courage to go to the cross on your behalf, not by being extra sweet to the disciples.

In fact, Scripture says that, "Greater love has no man than to give his life for a friend." The highest form of love is courage and self-sacrifice, a masculine virtue. You do not need society or a woman to give you value or identity. You don't need affirmation and acceptance from a woman. Femininity causes women to dance around issues to make sure everyone feels good, but Jesus was not shy about issues. He was direct and manly. God wanted it this way.

The Bible also says that "the head of a woman is man and the head of man is Christ." God put you in charge of the family for a reason, and that reason has to do with manliness. When you seek approval from a woman, you are violating the created order. Your approval should come from God. You should be proud of who you are. Only when you feel secure in who God has made you *as a man*, can you begin to cut away the addiction to needing a woman.

## BEING TOO EMOTIONAL

One of the side effects of the cultural loss of manliness is that many men have become over-emotional and never learned to control their negative emotions. We've taught our women not to cry and our men that they need to cry more. We've told our girls they should all play sports while letting our boys waste their lives away on computer games and porn. This leads to tough girls and weak men.

If this is you, then part of overcoming lust is developing some of the toughness that you missed. As a man, you are not supposed to get swept away in emotions. Speaking personally, my life experiences led me to be hyper-emotional. I felt like without a deep and powerful emotional connection or experience—to God, women, people—my life was meaningless. I eventually had to learn to turn this off. I realized that part of being man is being tough, and not being shaken up by all kinds of things that get thrown at me.

The idea of men being tough is continually mocked in popular culture today, and it was when I was growing up, so I thought it was stupid. Only on the journey of freedom did I discover it was truth. God intended you as a man to be strong and courageous, and not to be moved by challenges and adversity. You are a warrior, and God's demolition crew for the devil's kingdom. Die if you have to die, but don't whine about it.

Embracing this more stoic approach to life was a major key for me to living sober. I quit feeling tossed around, and emotionally needy, and started appreciating the glory of manliness.

## WHAT YOU ARE SEEKING

Sex is an act of worship. We worship what we crave. My experience is that most of what men are trying to get through sex falls into one of two broad categories: the need to feel loved, or the need to feel powerful. I believe these two needs are indicators of which aspect of your person you are trying to fulfill, either the masculine (power) or the feminine (love). If sex makes you feel powerful, then it's a sign that you are seeking to fulfill your sense of confidence as a man. If you are seeking love, then you are seeking approval and connection from women. What you seek reveals what is missing in your identity.

Your family structure and experiences growing up wire a lot of this in. These experiences set deep cues in your heart for what you will crave in sex. If you had experiences in your childhood that made you feel powerless or worthless, sex can be a world where you are a "god" who has power and authority, by having a woman submit or essentially worship you. For that brief time, you feel powerful, respected and manly. You need to discover the power of being a man– that you do not need approval from anyone else to be powerful and manly. God simply made you that way when he made you a man.

On the other hand, if you were not nurtured, did not have strongly comforting relationships, or were rejected in various ways, you might be seeking primarily love and connection from sex. You may actually have lots of love available to you in your life, but are probably unable to fully appreciate or experience it. Sex then presents a world where you can experience perfect "love" and acceptance by being desired by a woman. Becoming free involves learning to experience and appreciate non-sexual love from the people in your life.

I remember one man I met in a recovery group who was going through a life-threatening illness, but had started his freedom process years earlier. When he got sick, his wife and family gathered around him. He realized at that point how foolish he had been. He said, "If I hadn't changed my direction, I would have missed all of this." If your wife knows about your struggle and she is still with you, that's the proof-positive sign that she loves you much more than anyone you can fish up on the internet or your office. Jesus demonstrated what real love is not by coming along and doling out pleasure, but by being willing to suffer for us. Real love is demonstrated by being willing to endure hardship for someone else. Cleaning your receptors to receive this love is important.

Beneath each of the needs—for power and love— are deep beliefs about yourself that need ministry. If you are trying to get power needs met from sex, you have deep lies embedded in your heart that you need a woman's approval to be important. Perhaps key people in your life made you feel unimportant or powerless. If so, you need to attack these lies and begin to derive your value from the fact that you are God's son, created in

His image, and that he has made you to rule and reign over the earth. (Gen 1:28). You're not on the backseat of the bus. He made you "the head and not the tail" (Deut. 28:13). Lies at this level take time to get fully worked out of your personality. Proactively seek help from someone in ministry to overcome your sense of powerlessness.

Likewise if you are seeking a woman's approval or comfort, you most likely were not given strong messages to affirm your value as a man. The Bible says that "The head of a woman is man, and the head of a man is Christ" (1 Cor. 11:3). This means that you are supposed to be getting your approval from God not from a woman. He has made you to be strong and courageous and not to need approval from others all the time. That is part of your unique value as a man. Targeted ministry in this area will help you see the world differently. You will then be able to reject the lie that the woman's world is better, and instead realize your worth and value as a man.

# Application Questions

1. Do you feel like being a man is inferior to being a woman?

2. What elements of your personality are manly? Do you take pride in them or feel ashamed of them?

3. Was your family upside-down, with a dominant mother and a passive father? How did your family structure affect your craving for sex?

4. Do have people who love you, but yet you do not feel loved by it? Reflect on the love in your life and compare the long-term results of love to thrill.

# BUILD YOUR RELATIONSHIP WITH GOD

Sexual sin is ultimately a relationship problem. Its root cause is in the Garden of Eden when man was separated from God and from his wife. Sometimes we make the mistake of assuming that the entire fix is about our vertical relationship with God: but in reality, we have to work both vertically, and horizontally. Most of this book looks at the horizontal aspect of this problem, but in this chapter, I want to look at the vertical part: your relationship with God.

You need to develop a strong relationship with God in order to stay free, but some of our ideas about what that means are so far off target, that they almost guarantee continued bondage. When I first started to get aggressive about freedom, God made it very clear to me that I needed to change churches. On the surface, that seemed kind of irrelevant to me. I want to get free from lust, and you want me to change churches? But over time I have come to understand the wisdom in what God told me to do.

Although I considered myself a Spirit-filled Christian, who oriented his life around the things of God, and who believes in His perfect love, my subconscious understanding of God was much different. It was shaped by the much more rigid experiences I had had early in my Christian development, and by reading the Bible apart from an understanding of the love of God. Although there have been too many layers in this journey for me to unpack in this little booklet, I think it is important to highlight a couple of important points here.

Early on in this journey I attended a men's conference where the speaker preached a very powerful message about David and Bathsheba. It was heavy and very convicting. After inviting men to come down to the altar call, he promised them that if they came to the meeting the next day, he would give the secrets of freedom. Eager for answers, many came the next day. The speaker then told a story about a Korean man who read his Bible through many times a year. I can't remember how many times it was, but it was an astonishing amount. The moral of the story was: if you read your Bible (a lot) more, you will not fall into sin.

This story exemplifies the tendency in contemporary Christianity to look at the Bible as a magic solution to our problems. We think things like, "I fell into sin today because I didn't read my Bible," or "Are you struggling with temptation? Better read a couple of chapters." Now that I've been down the road a bit, I can say that this kind of thinking is actually an impediment to freedom. Reading the Bible certainly does help keep God's standard fresh in your heart, and the discipline of doing so regularly, like any discipline, is healthy for your self-control, but it's not magic.

## FOCUS ON RELATIONSHIP

After God has me change churches, I slowly came to realize that I had been promised to know God, but all I really knew was the Bible. You can know the Bible with what is in your head, but the process of knowing God has everything to do with what you know in your heart. Thinking primarily in terms of Bible reading or memory verses is actually an impediment to relationship, not a pathway to relationship.

Trying to bang out massive amounts of Bible reading is how you would relate to a schoolmaster or a drill instructor, not a loving father. Your focus must be on developing a relationship with God, not a relationship with the Bible. When you put the relationship first, and start thinking in terms of relationship, things change. Would you go a day without talking to a woman you were close to? Not if you want to keep the relationship strong. The same is true for God. Your first priority has to be spending time with Him. And not just any time, but time where you really open your heart and tell him what is going on, which is the second major issue.

## OPEN UP

A great deal of mainstream teaching implicitly teaches you not to open up and get real with God. This comes in many flavors: we do things like confess how righteous we are, tell God how horrible we are, ask for things, or repeat rote prayers. All of these are alike in the fact that they do not promote honesty and transparency in relationship. God is always wanting to be closer to you, and so a conversation with Him involves:

- Getting quiet enough to listen
- Being honest about where you are
- Being willing to change
- Being willing to obey

When you do these things, then your life when you are not actively focused on Him becomes a time of walking out what you worked on together. Developing this kind of relationship takes time bu tit is worth it. When you talk to God, He will talk back. Not through an audible voice, but through His Spirit speaking to your heart. You have to learn to tune in and listen to what He is saying.

When I used to fall into sin, I would go through what I would call a very "legal" process of praying the right prayer in order to clean my conscience to that I could feel better and move on. In other words, I was having a relationship with a law, not with a person. God had been explained to me primarily as a judge (albeit a loving one), so I related to Him that way. God doesn't want you to sin, apologize, and then go try to muscle it out alone until you sin again. He wants to speak to you day by day so that you can live free. Hiding from God is one of the root causes of sin, that's why He made Adam come out of hiding so He could deal with it. If you come out of hiding and talk to God each day, His love will sustain you.

Now, if I sin or start down the path of sin, I see it as a relationship problem. It's not a whole lot different than how you might see talking to your wife about it. I have disappointed someone who loves me, and who I love. I want to apologize and ask forgiveness, so that I can enjoy restored relationship  He forgives me and I return to fellowship. Then we can talk about what happened and what I can do to avoid it the next time. God is for you, not against you. He is the friend in your corner on the path to freedom. If you fight for the relationship, you'll be surprised how much less you have to fight the sin.

## WORSHIP FROM YOUR HEART

There is some faction of the Church that is aggressively afraid of emotions. We believe that emotions lie, so we cannot follow them. In fact, we probably shouldn't even have them. Build up your mind and follow it. This is a false idea which leads you to short circuit the emotional connection you are supposed to develop with God and with healthy people around you. You starve yourself of emotional connection and then, when you can't take it anymore, you have an intense emotional sex party.

Emotions are more like gauges on your dashboard. They indicate what is going on in your heart. If you feel depressed, for example, it's because of something you believe in your heart, and that belief is coming out in the form of negative emotions. Therefore you might have a bad emotion because you believed a lie, but the problem is not emotions, it's the lie. While being a disciplined and strong man is definitely going to require you to shut down and push past some emotions, it's is critical that in the important relationships of you life, you cultivate emotion, because that is how human beings were designed to connect to one another.

When my relationship with God is close, it *feels* close. I feel like I want him more, I feel His presence near me, I feel a deep love for Him and for others. These feelings are part of my bond to Him, built up over years of following him.

One important practice to developing this connection is to worship God through music. For many men this does not come easily and must be learned. Worship is not about repeating phrases or choruses. It is about allowing yourself to be carried away in your thoughts and emotions by a song. In order to do this, you need to find intense worship music like Bethel Music, where the worship leader is doing that. Don't worry about "praising Him," but allow the words to speak deeply to your identity and weak areas. The praise will come from your heart naturally. Along with that, inspiration is important. Sermons of people that inspire you, or reading of Christians who inspire you, need to be part of your regular diet to stay on track with God. At the same time, when I feel oppressed and challenged, I like to turn on intense Black Gospel music and make the declarations of a warrior.

These kinds of processes are designed to keep your connection to God living and active. It's not a one time event. It's a lifelong process of abiding in the vine. My pastor said once that life is like going to the grocery store—if you go in hungry, everything looks good no matter how bad it is for you, and eventually you will eat something. If you are not living full of God, nothing else you do is going to matter, you're going to have to eat something that is not good for you to stay full.

Explaining all the ins and outs of developing a relationship with God is far beyond the scope of this book, but if these few breadcrumbs spoke to you, then you are probably in need of a paradigm shift like I was when God confronted me. I suggest you read my book *No Exit: Finding Jesus in the Maze of Religion,* where I go into detail about building a healthy relationship with God. You might need to change churches, music, or even friends. You might need to reignite your relationship with God from a new perspective. Although I can't explain all that here, if you seek God and follow the breadcrumbs He's leaving you, He will show you. If you're doing it right, over time you should develop a strong bond of love between you and God which will form a strong barrier to sin.

## Application Questions

1.  Do you approach your problem with God as legal or a relational issue? Ask God what He thinks about your struggle.

2.  Do you enjoy time with God, or is it a chore? What is hindering your relationship with God? Your friends, your particular church, bad ideas? What do you need to change in order to be closer to Him?

3.  Start the process of developing an emotional relationship with God. Choose a time, place, or quiet activity like walking, that you can do every day where you can get real with God and hear His voice guide you through the freedom process. Incorporate worship through music.

# THINK LIKE A WINNER

There is something about the sexual struggle which makes it all consuming, even once you start going sober. One of the biggest traps in escaping lust as a Christian man is what I call the "death spiral." You fall into sin, so you hate yourself; and then since you hate yourself, so you fall into sin again. This cycle repeats over and over again as things become worse and worse.

You simply cannot defeat lust in this kind of mindset. Even if you are having major sexual issues, do not allow it to become the center and meaning of your life. You will destroy yourself. The fact is that you become what you behold. The more you focus on sin, the more trapped you become in it. God has made you much more than a porn-head. God has a purpose for your life and wants to do amazing things through you. And to be honest, what I have observed in my life and in the lives of others around me is that He will begin to do these amazing things about the same time you start down the road of purity in a serious way. He doesn't wait until you are totally free to move in your life. He walks right alongside you just like Jesus did with the disciples.

Therefore you need to declare war on the death spiral. Getting free is a big challenge, but it is not hopeless. When you tell yourself that it is hopeless, you are putting the padlock on your own cell. When you tell yourself that you are worthless because of your struggle with porn, that becomes a self-fulfilling prophecy. Allow God to forgive you and start believing in yourself again.

Remind yourself of the great things He is doing and wants to do through your life.

I cannot stress how important all of this is. You cannot allow your crusade for freedom to be a negative adventure about how messed up you are and how addicted you are. The main story of your life is not sex, it's your relationship with God. The main story of your life is not defeat, it is how God is leading you to victory. You have hope, a purpose, and a future. You must get this truth deep inside of yourself before you will be successful in your quest for freedom.

## SUCCESS

The more you focus on women and sex, the more you will want them. Part of what gets broken inside of you as a man when you indulge in sexual pursuits is your sense of self-worth, and your pursuit of Godly success. Our upside-down culture has taught men to be hyper-emotional and told Christian men that seeking success is ungodly, and the result is that we are seeking these hyper-emotional encounters with women that are not designed to fulfill us.

As a man, you were not made to survive without any sense of purpose. It is popular in the church today to tell us we should "be" rather than "do," but that is just another way that feminine values have replaced manliness in our culture. It is not the message Jesus gave. For Him the two things went together: "Abide in me and you will bear much fruit." Build your relationship with Him and that will lead to exciting results and action. You were not made to live without a sense of success. You need more than to know that God loves you—you need to know that He is going to help you be successful for Him. These are feelings that you need as a man, and that you will find very fulfilling.

I have found that as I have developed a stronger sense of God's purpose in my life, I have wanted porn less and less. I don't need to get value and meaning from a fantasy because I am experiencing it in my real life. This is because my manly need for success is being met. We often think that porn is filling a void for relationship, but it can just as easily fill a void for purpose and meaning. When you set goals for yourself, and more importantly, when you see the hand of God working in your life, showing His favor on you, that can make a huge difference in your pursuit of purity. I have learned that pursuing Godly success is a powerful antidote to pursuing women. As a man, I am supposed to be focused on the mission God gave me in the Garden: to "take dominion" (Gen 1:28).

## WINNING THOUGHTS

Maybe you're in a place right now where literally everyone thinks you are a scumbag, including yourself. I know how brutal it is to have to confess sin to friends and associates. It feels like a bottomless pit of worthlessness. Somehow you have become the made-for-TV nightmare that no one wants anything to do with. You have to know that no matter what anyone else thinks, if you have repented, God has forgiven. Not only has he forgiven, but he has erased it, because "As distant as the east is from the west, that is how far he has removed our sins from us." (Psalm 103:12).

You need to begin to look at yourself differently. You are a victor and not a victim. You were losing in the past because you were not practicing one or more of the keys in this book, and Satan ate your lunch, but today is a new day. It may take time for the people around you to see you differently, and maybe some of them never will adjust, but God has cleaned your conscience, and He is the one who really matters. As you agree with Him, your life will change.

God has made you "the head and not the tail" (Deut 28:13). He has made you "more than a conqueror" (Rom 8:37). He has made you a champion and given you a purpose in life. You might not be feeling it right now, but I promise he has great things for you on the other side if you will push all the way through this struggle and do not quit. Your life is not over. God has a way of restoring things you've lost and giving you upgrades for things that he can't restore.

Sexual struggle is not who you are. It's a symptom of living disconnected from God. You are not an alien for having this struggle. Most men in our culture have significant challenges in this area, but you are choosing to fight it instead of giving in. When the thoughts come to you don't replay a tape of discouragement as if this is what your life is about. Tell the devil that you are getting a divorce and that you want God no matter what. Then turn to God and begin to trust that he can overcome even the strongest foe.

# Application Questions

1. Have you allowed the quest for sexual purity to define who you are? What does a victorious mindset say instead?

2. What negative feelings about yourself and baggage are you carrying from the struggle for sexual purity?

3. Where can you get value in your life other than fantasy? Write down some of the things God is doing or wants to do in your life.

# THE PATHWAY TO PURITY

I remember as a teenager feeling incredibly discouraged that I would be fighting this hopeless battle my entire life – at the very least for 10 years or so until I got married. The whole idea of quitting forever was very daunting and not a very realistic starting place. We love to tell each other stories about how we just quit sin or got fixed overnight, because it encourages us that God can do miracles, but honestly most real-life stories of people with deep problems don't go that way. In fact, I've known men who were able to quit smoking or drinking in one day, but who still struggled to overcome lust for many years.

Setting basically impossible goals is only going to discourage you more. Jesus is looking for absolute surrender, not absolute perfection. If you walk with Him one step at a time, He will get you free. Therefore, start by setting realistic goals for yourself. Here are some phases that you may find helpful:

**Cut the Cord.** The very first thing you should do is shut down all of your access to pornography by installing filters, or accountability software on your phone and PC. Right along with that, you should open up to someone who you know loves you about your problem. This may be difficult, but the exact reason that this is difficult is what is going to help you get free. I'm not saying you won't fall again, but you have to start building up "clean time." Your focus during this phase is explicitly on eliminating all external sources of sin

I have found that "One Clean Week" is a great way to set goals. Set your goal for one week specifically without porn. If you're ultra-addicted, you might need to set the goal even lower but for most people starting out, one clean week is doable, even though difficult. You will have to white knuckle through it to get there. You might have to really work hard not to be alone or start a new hobby, but be a man and do whatever it takes to hit the milestone! If you speak in tongues, this can help you in some of the hardest times.

This process could take a while before it starts to become achievable, and you will have many steps and discoveries along the way, but this is a great first goal.

**Masturbation.** Once you are at a place where you are getting a clean week without porn pretty consistently. You're ready to push the next level: masturbation. I'm not saying that you should be masturbating in the first phase, but I'm just helping you with where to focus. Quitting masturbation can be really hard, because most men have been masturbating their entire lives. It's become more like a way of life than a habit. Repeat the same process. Go for "One Clean Week" without porn or masturbation. You will have to make lifestyle changes to do this, applying everything you learned in this book.

For many men, this is like losing a friend, because of the chemicals involved. The hormones released when you ejaculate cause you to bond, but since there is no one there, you become bonded to the act itself. Therefore, when you stop, you may go through a phase of grief like a breakup. You may feel lonely for the first time in a long time. You will have to learn to fill your loneliness with healthier things.

**Fantasies.** If you are able to break the masturbation chain, you're really making good progress, but you're not there yet. When you cut the pornography and masturbation you may find that you have a heightened desire for women, are more sensitive to things like ads on the internet. You really have to get your thought life to total purity if you want to maintain your freedom. The hardest part about this is that daily life is going to present you with triggers to fantasize. At this point, the three main kinds of triggers are:

- **Women You Know.** If you get too close, you are likely to want to fantasize about them. If you are married, put up boundaries that keep you from getting this close.

- **Women You See**. If you meet a woman you find unusually attractive it can get you going. When this happens, you should clear your heart and repent right away, rather than letting it plant a seed.

- **Media other than porn**. Although you have cut porn, all kinds of other media can stir the pot. Honestly, the less media you are exposed to, the better.

You need to get to the place where none of these triggers lead you to fantasize. When you start racking up clean weeks not fantasizing, you are starting to live like a free man.

Sobriety is a process of keeping every lustful thought out of your heart. At first, you are fighting a raging forest fire, but with work, you will be able to get the blaze down. An amazing thing happens when you learn to keep every lustful thought out: your sexual system shuts down. Instead of being always one moment away from a fall, you can go weeks without any significant feelings of temptation. Because you live in the world, you will have little encounters that tempt to start the engine again through fantasy, but be aware, once you start pouring gas on the fire, it's going to flame up again.

What you learn to do instead is when you have encounters that tempt you to lust, clean them out of your heart quickly before the fire starts flaring up and the motor starts running. I put my energy toward manly things and healthy relationships instead of fantasies. Seeing this process at work has helped me to truly understand why Jesus puts his finger on lustful thoughts not just behavior. If you keep your heart clean, the chemical fire won't start, and you'll get used to being sober all the time.

**Love.** The final phase is for you to develop a true redemptive and protective heart toward women. Hopefully you have been moving in this direction all along, but when you have cut the fantasies to the point where you're not actively sinning in your mind, you still have to come around the corner to be proactively loving. This cannot be done simply by human effort. It takes an ongoing connection with God and renewal of your mind, because you live in a fallen world. As you maintain this heart, you start to look at the inner person rather than the outer. Your one clean week is caring about each female you encounter equally with love like a sister, mother, or daughter. Having a heart of blessing, rather than a heart of consuming.

My experience is that these phases naturally overlap one another. As you push for victory over porn, you are naturally going to start masturbating less, which will lead you into the next phase. As you push for victory over masturbation, you are going to have to fantasize less, leading you into the next phase, etc. By breaking this into phases, I'm not saying that any kind of sin is OK. You will still have to repent whenever you sin. I'm simply saying that by setting your goals at a realistic level for where you are, you will have much greater success for the total victory you crave.

## 25-24-21

Because you are dealing with a drug that is built into your body, the process of gaining victory is a lot like detoxing from a drug. If you dwell on lustful thoughts, you will get a dose of the drug, and then you will want more, so you will be tempted to think about it more, and the natural tendency is for things to escalate until you act on it with porn and masturbation.

You can stop the cycle once it is started, however. I think about with a simple rule of 25-24-21. If you stop thinking lustful thoughts completely, after 25 minutes your body will drop from high alert down to a more manageable state. This first hurdle is the most psychologically important, because if you have not acted out in a long time, the hit of drugs to your mind is so powerful that it can feel like it is hopeless to resist. But set that goal of 25 minutes for your body to calm back down to normal. Do something super-distracting. I generally do not endorse video games, but this is a case where in an emergency they can be helpful: to put your mind on something totally engrossing and let the physical aspects catch up. Pushups can be very helpful in changing your body chemistry in the moment as well.

But you're not out of the clear yet. Your next goal is to make it until the next day "24 hours" without feeding it. You should proactively turn away from it in your heart and toward God and proactively think protective thoughts about women instead of lustful thoughts. After 24 hours clean, you are going to start to go back to "normal."

But the fact is that by feeding it you did plant a seed that will linger in the back of your mind for some time, and will tempt you to feed it again until you push up against the edge again. This is where the third phase comes in: 21 days. If you make it 21 days without feeding the lustful thoughts, you will find that it is really in the back of your mind and life. This third leap is not easy, but it's important to realize that getting does make a difference. Just playing "touch and go" every few days keeps you in the cycle of trouble. You need to get to long periods where you think no lustful thoughts at all.

Do not make the mistake of thinking that you will beat it all in one attempt, or that if you fail, you shouldn't try again. Remember Jesus honors your commitment to purity. The goal is more important than the number of attempts it takes to get there.

## Application Questions

1. What do you need to do to get your next "Clean Week."? Consider all of the tools you have learned in this book

2. Are you practicing living sober in your mind? What is going to be your habit going forward when you experience temptation that is outside of your control?

3. Consider how to address other areas that underlie or play into your long-term freedom— i.e. personal or marriage counseling, changing churches or certain beliefs, etc.

www.ingramcontent.com/pod-product-compliance
Lightning Source LLC
Chambersburg PA
CBHW071828020426
42331CB00007B/1645